WINSTON the TRAVELING DOG

goes to PERU & ARGENTINA

by
Cynthia Anne
Finefrock

©2023 Cynthia Anne Finefrock

All rights reserved. No part of this publication may be reproduced in any form without the express written permission of the author. For permission requests contact cfinefrock@gmail.com.

This is a work of fiction. Any resemblance to actual events or persons, living or dead, is entirely coincidental.

Faithful Friends Publishing
ISBN 978-1-7369459-2-6 (hardcover)
ISBN 978-1-7369459-5-7 (paperback)
Vectors by Adobe Stock
First Edition

CynthiaAnne.com

This book belongs to
_____

and is a gift from
_____

Winston's Travel Photos

This is Winston — a furry, energetic, and travel-OBSESSED Pomeranian from the USA. It's safe to say that after two trips overseas, Winston had caught the travel bug.
A year had already flown by since his trip to Egypt and Jordan, and Winston was itching for another ADVENTURE. Where could he go with exotic animals, breathtaking scenery, and delicious food? From the pictures he'd seen on the Travel Channel, South America seemed like a good fit!

After months of planning, the big day arrived.
Winston was off to Peru and Argentina!

After a very long flight, Winston arrived in Peru and went straight to baggage claim. He waited and waited and waited. His luggage was nowhere to be found! "Oh my DOG..." thought Winston. "My luggage is missing! What am I supposed to do without my bones, toys, and clothes?!"

"No time to whimper," Winston decided. "It's time to go shopping!"

Winston wanted to support the local shop owners, so he bought a handmade Peruvian PAWncho. It was perfect to wear to Machu Picchu, a well-preserved Inca civilization.

Located in the Andes Mountains, Machu Picchu is 7,000 feet above sea level! Good thing Winston isn't afraid of heights!

While exploring Machu Picchu, Winston stumbled upon some llamas. Winston learned that Incas valued llamas for their wool and nutrient-dense poop. He couldn't believe it! Llamas were praised for their poop, yet he was always getting in trouble for leaving his around the house. Talk about unfair!

Winston's next stop in Peru was the Amazon Rainforest. The Amazon is the world's largest rainforest, spanning over eight countries! It was very hot and humid in the rainforest. Winston was panting by the time he arrived at his hotel.

UH-OH,

more bad news...first his luggage was lost and now the hotel had lost his reservation! "Stay calm. It's going to be okay," Winston reassured himself. Luckily, he was able to quickly book a room at a nearby lodge. To Winston's surprise, this lodge was even better than the one he had originally booked!

There was another dog staying at the lodge, too: a Golden Retriever from Colorado! They decided to go on a hike through the rainforest together.

There were many interesting plants and insects to see in the rainforest, which makes sense since the Amazon is home to over three million species. The trees were also very tall. So tall, in fact, that Winston couldn't get ahold of any sticks to chew...

The Amazon was AMAZ-ing! Winston couldn't wait to come back to Peru someday, but for now, he was excited to see what Argentina had in store for him!

The next morning, Winston arrived at the airport and found out his flight to Buenos Aires was cancelled. Winston had been looking forward to visiting the capital of Argentina, but what's a pup to do?!

WELCOME TO ARGENTINA

He looked at a map of Argentina and decided to buy a plane ticket to Iguazú Falls instead. He had been wanting to buy a new raincoat, and this was the perfect excuse!

IGUAZU FALLS

After arriving in Iguazú National Park, Winston learned that Iguazú Falls isn't just one waterfall; it's actually 275 different ones! Iguazú means "big water" and Winston had to agree, Iguazú Falls was huge!

Coati usually travel in large groups called bands. Winston was hoping they would let him be a part of their band, but they were too busy trying to find food to notice him. Winston decided to follow them anyway. He wasn't one to miss out on a good lunch.

After enjoying the tropical climate of the rainforest, Winston traded his raincoat for winter gear. His last stop in Argentina was Perito Moreno Glacier.

Winston learned that Perito Moreno is one of the only glaciers in the world that isn't shrinking!

WOW!

Since glaciers are made of freshwater, the water on the glacier was so pure you could drink it. "It's like one big doggy bowl!" Winston exclaimed. "Speaking of doggy bowls, is it dinner time yet? Glacier trekking makes me hungry!"

For dinner, Winston attended a traditional Bark-B-Q. There were many different kinds of meats to try, all paired with a green sauce called chimichurri. He also ate grilled cheese, called provoleta, and pastries stuffed with savory ingredients, called empanadas.

He ended the day with a horseback ride through Patagonia. It sure was beautiful!

That night, as Winston fell asleep with a full belly, he dreamed about all the amazing places he traveled to in South America. Although things didn't always go as planned, Winston learned the importance of being flexible. He also realized that when things don't go your way, staying positive helps. Something even better may be waiting for you! In Winston's case, it was a closet full of new clothes, an unexpected friendship, and an opportunity to visit one of the prettiest waterfalls in the world.

Next time, though, Winston plans to pack a carry-on suitcase...
Just in case...

THE END.

Until next time...

If you enjoyed this or any book in the Winston the Traveling Dog series, kindly leave a review on Amazon or Goodreads. Your support of Indie Authors is always greatly appreciated.

Cynthia Anne Finefrock lives with her family in Scottsdale, Arizona, in the United States.

Cynthia's true passion is experiencing as much of the world as possible through the lens of her camera. After designing a website to showcase her diverse photography, Cynthia decided to edit her dog Winston into her travel landscapes. What started as a comical exchange between friends has transpired into an award-winning book series.

Before she ventured into the world of writing children's books, Cynthia graduated from the University of Southern California before obtaining her Masters in Physician Assistant Studies from Cornell University. In her free time, Cynthia enjoys cooking, playing with her dogs, and researching new travel destinations.

Stay connected:
Website: CynthiaAnne.com
Instagram: @WinstonTravels_
Facebook: @WinstontheTravelingDog

Made in the USA
Las Vegas, NV
21 March 2025